To Marg

W

with best wishes.

Max Reater

23rd Nov, 1998

Winter Fires

Max Plater

TORONTO

Exile Editions
1998

This edition is published by Exile Editions Limited,
20 Dale Avenue, Toronto, Ontario, Canada M4W 1K4

Sales Distribution:
McArthur & Company
c/o Harper Collins
1995 Markham Road
Toronto, Ontario
M1B 5M8
800 387 0117

Layout and Design by *MICHAEL P. CALLAGHAN*
Composed and Typeset at *MOONS OF JUPITER,* Toronto
Printed and Bound by *AMPERSAND PRINTING,* Guelph
Cover Painting by *FRANCO BONETTI*
Author's Photograph by *BRIAN DERRICK*

The Canada Council
Conseil des Arts du Canada

The publisher wishes to acknowledge the assistance toward publication of the Canada Council and the Ontario Arts Council.

ISBN 1-55096-250-7

Acknowledgements

Some of these poems have appeared in *Verve, Quarter Moon Quarterly, Undertow, Pemmican, Amethyst Review* and *Writer's Publishing* .

for

James J. McAuley

with many thanks

Contents

I

Absence

in memory of Frances Sears

On cold mornings of absence
birds that used to sing take flight
or hide silently under shadows
where the trees ignore them.

In leaves not far from my face
a sudden movement of light
indicates a bird I had not seen
has just flown away.

Bone River

I loved you like the earth.
I stood at the ravine and wept.
I feel still, the pull
of water, cool and constant
over and around the clacking rocks,
the spray in my hair.

I will go with the pulses of water,
to the child born within myself,
the life I once held.

Life is momentary like regret,
a flash of fish scale in white water,
a splinter caught in flesh.

My rose-thorn bones have no desire
for this skin, this appeasement.
Lips are of little use to me. The body
sags under the weight of these old
splayed bones, fingers crumbling where bone
shoots out its messages.

I want life like wind in the hand,
or pearled light on the edge of a fern
trembling with rain, the texture of a leaf
prickly damp in an upturned palm. I want

to walk at night by the lake,
break the black water with my arms
and drink the liquid stars.

For now I'll sit in the shade,
fill myself with the breath of flowers
and listen to the river crashing
deep into crevices of stone.

The rocks of the river
are my mother and my father.

Intuit

From webs of silk nothing
breaks through oblivion like a spoon.

The mind's exactions attract
upsurges through the whirling epicentre

human forms absorb in abruptions and diagonals,
ambiguities of phase and dolor criss-

crossed in praise and colour,
threads of hours and days breaking

in arteries of jewelled weather
where river flows to bone.

Angels

They appear in stippled stones under shining water,
as sunset lights skittering across a lake.
As leaves on the woodland floor lift and float
for a firefly second they light the air.

In filtered light through butterfly's wings, they
come
quietly, a breathing echo of minute wings upon the
ear.
In the light of an eagle's eye they linger,
elusive living elements of the dead.

They quiver on the wall in flower faces, wake
a child from sleep with yellow light and laughter,
rock him with a grandparent's assurance, carry him
in the arms of gods across a slow river.

They come as eager eyes in hedgerows,
eyes that only the slow-eyed child can know.
Eyes that follow a schoolboy home from school
and watch the detailed lives of children.

Stars

Nebulae of your numeric eyes
sturdy as banked clouds
forsaken, staring

into blank nothings, your eyes
lost to trig points
astronomers do not know. Silent

inversion of inkblots, indecipherable as snow
apprehended from silence
with a vow vaporised.

Incalculable sum of what
on earth cannot be done to wriggling
sperm, uncanny fingerlings

circling the planets in avoidant bursts,
adroit manoeuverings of
sustaining energy to last out the last

pegs of breath pinned
and bridled with shining metallic
stings in the skin, injecting all

but you in your lunar blue dimension, singing
in every tongue, every declension,
every last stream of milky sky

before the magi squeeze
the heart's last juices
riding light into the world.

Seahorse

for Amber

When the moon is curled as a lip
in the silhouette of an apple tree
I think of you as embryo, the seahorse
sleeping in the sea of your mother. Floating
almost motionless in the sea which is
and will always be your mother.

We scarcely knew you then,
a splinter of dust caught on flesh.
Swelling, you drew closer, larger until
your heart thumped fast in pre-birth strength.
We could feel you tremble like fruit,
a throbbing globe of water, the moon
in its full white orb.

Dreaming with Amber in My Arms

for Amber

Pebbles are larger under my feet.
The body sways to balance them.
Sea winds thicken in my hair.
Little hands pull them across my face.
Seagulls still awake are making beds of air
and I, falling to sea through sleep
grope the wind for your face.

I wake to starlight
glancing the surface of your eyes.
My newborn daughter gazing
silent, breathing the after-midnight air.

African Sky

for Trevor

The shaman sings of roses
to a leopard skin sky

and the light that fills his eyes
falls slowly in the slanted vision

of striped and shuttered night;
All things are shadow and light.

There is a beast which looks like a zebra,
grazes just under the eyes

and nibbles gently at your sleep.

Night Horses

for Trevor

Secrets of a thousand cloudy children
with shining eyes and faces full of chocolate
on a journey the mind takes —
its five wise men flying into night,
of horses and losses and small dimensions.
The children dream holding
the air in their arms, the air of dreams.

What an infant they find in a field of animals.
What light on the hooves of the white
horses chasing around a stable
in the rain-soaked night
and the rain-soaked morning.
The children dream gathering
the air in their arms, the air of flight.

Are there places where the rain
falls forever gently forgetting to stop
and the child rides a white horse
bareback through endless space
to a place larger than time?
The children dream flying:
the air in their arms knows no time.

Winter Storm

for Judi

I hear your heart thudding into sleep,
the hollow thud of a bucket trailing in a well,
the long plunge into water, echo of bucket on rock,
see the black water brimmed with stars.

As you lie waking in the new day
you speak my name from sleep. Beyond
the light pulsing in curtain folds, snow
has changed the features of our world.

Enclosures

for Judi

Somewhere your lips enclose
a thief in frost upon the window
and as beautifully as your fingers
close I find what I cannot find
to free these moments.

Love is all is all and you are what
you are and I alone except for this
momentary echo only one or two
words away, one or two movements
toward another form of consciousness.

Love in a blizzard of wings takes
what remains of these uneven things
softly into the heart of snow.

Between Us

for Judi

Above dry canyons where our worlds meet
not one word is lost between us.

We step across them on a string bridge.

As You Are

for Judi

As lovely as you are to me
bathed in God's blue fountains,
further than you are from me
in my deepest shadows
the inverted telescope sings
and my petty world
jigs to its tunes.

Further than you reach I feel
what it is in all this
childish bliss that sets the sidewalks
at an angle,
and criss-crosses with trails of blood
the upturned mountains.

Rough Love

for Judi

Your answers wait: *avanti: arriba* —
falling down to love with rubber arms,
perfume and potions reducing
will to feather, waking inert momentary pulses,
jungle hormones, impetuous drummings,
leaving untouched the rumpled parts —
the roughness of rough love,
unsanded oak hearts of what could be
ultimate art. We're human yet
and riddle each other with fantasy,
never becoming enough of what we love.

Dusk On Barnston Island

for Trevor and Amber

Through the haze of buttercups
light rises
along the restless contours of a horse

thrusting in shadows through the long grass
reflected curves and turns
in bursts of topaz.

Beneath the spires of cottonwoods
the cotton floats in shafts of evening air
drifting into eyes of cyclists

spinning on a sudden
edge of the glazed river shuddering
towards the Georgia Straight.

Because of what you've lost
today the sun scoops up two silhouettes
of children racing home on bikes

beneath an avenue of trees.
Through telescopic sight the sun
in concentrated flame on ochre flesh

unbinds two shadows in the fire
igniting features stretching into vagaries
so they are lost to who they were

and come about to face again
the sun with faces of fire
and the earth turning inside them.

II

Acceleration

Kubla Khan or Kubler-Ross, does it really matter?
Right-footed and left-brained each player struts
accelerating up the freeway of his life
and brakes on matter running out
of cash and gas, the dash
becoming rust, and running
with a shaking spear
impales acrostics hidden by de Vere,
but cannot piggyback across
the backs of dead ideas.
Yeah man, life's an itch so whether you
scratch it or not
(ay, there's the rub),
it speeds you up and pumps out blood,
bleeds and keeps on bleeding.

Youth enters with McPherson Struts
and revving up a kool stampede of horses —
chrome under black metallic snorting,
cranks the woofers raising his alarum for the dead,
and on his tattooed skin a stripper sings
strutting biceps in blue ink
and shivering her nubiles as he
rounds a corner, bottoms on a hump
and exits at the speed of night and leaves

old farts at forty far behind
at green lights waiting for a change
blithering into dust wondering
which which is which.
                                        Kubla Khan
or Kubler-Ross, it doesn't really matter.
Mind's over matter tapping out
on a thirsty road a thousand ways of being.
Pleasure Dome or Hospice,
Emperor of Xanadu or Doctor of the Dying
dying from and into matter,
what matters is the mind. So never mind
if you're stranded car-less in Inuvik.
It's not a license so you can't renew it.

From our first breath it's the air that kills,
fills us up with dust and drives us in reverse.

Empty

I rent obscurity by the hour
with nickels and dimes that fall
on my tin-roofed brain

while the rain pours inside me.
With a future and a giggle
a skip and a gaggle,

I am off to nowhere
skating in a universal feeling
and feeling nothing, I fall.

I wrestle life like a drunk
dancing with a tin can
and the emptiness inside it

is what I am.

Prisoner of the Page

The sky is heavy with eyelids
and the tired feet of prisoners
clap like the hooves of a million
horses hammering through my head.

I am the vine and the wine,
the lonely and sublime,
the maker and consumer,
the lover and the bed.

I dangle on my elbows over books,
eyes falling quarters spinning in to look.
I am alone in a bowl of death
eaten daily by a giant.

To reach the high window
I stand on imaginary shoulders
to look out from the prison of this page
at the pulsing contours of the day.

Violent Genesis

The blood cries doubled in its sleep,
embattled memory plunging
so many scalpels,

everything severed without effort
cries out of itself
to another world where

citizens of the primal state scream
the world is on fire
for the undiscovered dead.

Over tombs of lost cadavers
and pythons of sleep
the poisoned teeth of millions

drool through purple tides, and tongues
strung with fruit
are impaled by Adam on a shark's tail

spurring into granite.
In prison clouds a thousand eyes
look out through barbed sun, barbed rain,

through a vestibule of hope
and are afraid.
And so the hands grow closer

as consciousness becomes
a kind of forgetting,
a trap you set and blame another.

Feathers

The man in the sports car is dead.
Racing down the hill
he failed to stop at the stop sign
and slammed a semi loaded with chickens
turning it on its side.
Feathers and cages of fifteen hundred
chickens scattered across
the intersection. A man crushed
and the mind's filled with white feathers
gliding over grass and trees,
settling like blown snow
on the black road, as wind-whipped chickens
screech from overturned cages,
claws scratching at metal
and feathers flying everywhere.

Heart Attack

Pivot and squeeze
of the iron lung pumps
indigenous and dumb the daily minutes
rumbling to mechanical tunes,
penumbra and disaster.

The wound ticks, clocking
from loss its advantage,
chuckling into veins
hieroglyphic drum-taps
of fluid in skin, of fever and coma.

Death comes up through the wound
dark-veined and surgical
spooning holes in air,
cutting into black turf
the iced contours of breath.

Cold
into the cold north waiting,
Heaven takes its turn.

Death Has A Language Of Its Own

1.

Death has a language of its own.
It listens on the telephone, slips
through pinholes in skin, angelic
anaesthetic, mute and mumbled.
Death breathes obscenities in you,
swims your stagnant pools as a tadpole.
Let him drown fiercely who dares
double-cross death in a second language.
You babble its name in rubble and shadow.
You're a trouble sale baby, you jumble and fumble
with muddy fingers, you dribble and dabble,
fish with your finger in a puddle.
You play with this masquerade as if
the substance of death were somewhere else.

2.

Death is a language of blood and bone.
It feeds at the edges of the known, sips
from your eyes by the hour, eats the corn
of flesh with ease and innocence.
Let this cannibal eat, rat-hearted tadpole.
After the first taste you'll ask for more.
You'll bite through death and emerge
somewhere on the other side of words
with the cow who jumped over the moon,
the cat, the fiddle and little Boy Blue.
Death does not require belief, observe the body
toenails and follicles dying as they grow.
Death's soft nose rests on your shoes
and waits to eat whatever you choose.

3.

Death is a language of incantation,
of spells chanted in innocence
springing in a canticle of breath,
subterfuge squeezed from a toothpaste tube,
bitten thoughts splashing into words,
syllables of logic swirling to abort.
Each impulse nixed as it runs like a
mouse through the wainscot. The Cat
licks his claws. Death severs every cord
to spinning invocation, circles in circles
in lineal time, all sweat dripping dry
crying, "God, use me like a savage.
I'm lost in salt. My tongue
feeds itself but nothing else."

Heaven

in memory of Mavis Flanders

Through ceremonies of riddles and bloodlines
riding the body's tides

through fields of fact
the spilt miles of white bones

measure the lost infrequent hopes
of blistering tongues.

Are there no myths
to mother us,

to wheel
our helpless bodies through the centuries,

no gestures of darkness uncurling
in moist hands

to help the feet step lightly
as the heart reaches its ultimate pulse?

Are there no easy deceptions
this side of paradise, no steps to Heaven

only a doorway
to and from the heart?

After

After a thousand days there came a thousand deaths.
Each man sang for his supper in silence
under white sun, sentences

leaping inward on a thin thread of fire.
Trees which gave no shade
filled with birds

who came, saw, and never sang,
their wings beating the haze of perforated distance.
Ghosts in empty teacups exploded

as snow whirled over stooped survivors,
hot coloured snow,
a kaleidoscope emptying from space

and schoolchildren's hands were covered with the particles,
the colours, the fast twitching.
In boughs of oaks

burnt leaves curled back like cat's tongues
and spat.

All the fallen leaves of trees were rushing to the sun.

III

Rain on the Mountains: Ghazals

I

Over coasts of cold gestures the eye of a tiger
flares into the sky.

White-brained and logical
with handshakes for rattlesnakes;

outpost of an unknown language,
the white rain saying

through tongues of water,
blue ridges sinking.

Don't fold or bend
just mutilate at each end;

the wound at the end of the world swallows in one
great gulp

all previous moments.

II

Into the mouths of stars
tongue-tipped light.

Nibbling at time on an antique table,
you are older than your wishes;

reducing your shadow by a pound or two;
flesh bleached out with reason.

Little worms ripple on sand
like question marks.

Wolves of flesh
linger among sparse saplings.

III

To work and die, but in the end
it's dying that counts.

Turning tables on times tables:
one times one has been asking for it.

Riding a jet carpet through the air,
arriving on time for time.

Through the zig zags of discourse,
gravity fills like a sponge.

Time sits in the body; a knife
bound by a wound.

IV

Five horsemen of apocalypse
bite their tongues riding into fire

wearing the world to ribbons,
shredding milleniums, trampling mountains.

In the furnace of an hour, the rushing breath of
horses,
ghosts rising from beer glasses;

archdukes of the blood, assassination in their eyes
implode from blades of bayonets.

Sarajevo rutted in winter light,
heavy guns thrubbing up against the backdrop

of a body clothed in frost,
all the unseen vertebra broken.

How do you tell others how
to break the wings of ice between their shoulders?

V

To execute one moment
with a shot.

From either side I'm human,
only the middle's gone;

went without me knowing,
didn't feel a thing.

The parts we keep alive
by feast or fasting.

Rancour so quick to show
in elbows and x-rays and arithmetic;

little Brutus's stabbing the blood
with bile and vengeance.

The night a dark grenade
whispers revenge.

VI

In a calabash of ashes
I see you sewn in sack cloth.

In midnight's acre against unbalanced ends,
the moon strikes ten.

Horses in flame
run riderless through the night.

Arteries melt in a blind man's bluff
of plastic explosives;

straight as a breakfast of arrows
candle-tongued and taciturn.

Love is in the body. It is not
a foreign object.

VII

So many pinched years
squeezed from a few dry saints;

symbols that pass like urine
daily through its circuitry and vents.

On fresh soil
shadows hide their appetites.

Tiny tree toads, lily-pad Carusos
keep the neighbours awake.

Beneath the webbed toes of shadows
iron feet can't save them.

VIII

The half-beat sings to itself
where the single bullet waits for a cell.

Abysmal minor consolations of
compass or forged tongue.

In winged flutterings
liquid contradictions reflected;

the pull of surf;
slow extortion of water.

Is anyone out there
still alive?

IX

Betrayal becomes a thousand tongues
licking at the feet;

the hammer of mortality
heavy in the eyes;

incendiary seed;
magnetic lovers torn from polarity;

a cynic's lexicon, faithless lesson.
I hunch down into myself breathing sand;

a broken hand
on the edge of nowhere;

the stitch
that is always language.

X

Crying to gravity;
a wolf afraid of air.

A spark eating the edges
of night.

Star following blood;
the dark fledgling seasons.

Unicorn afraid of what he might
do with a razor.

The DNA hissing at itself;
a fatal gland wilting in its shadow.

Chained to your abyss I sing
a sinew in a season.

XI

I'm a perfect liar;
some days I mop the sun with a sponge.

A spider crawls
endlessly up and down my spine.

Someone spilled plutonium on my feet.
I wiped them clean. Death

a la mode
is a piece of cake.

If I were the father of failure
I'd invent myself.

XII

Bedeviled rain falling on pure thoughts;
aquatic syntax at edge of light.

Pine singing through its knots
strains against the scree;

winding and unwinding
like a bent son.

The wet-headed sun
swims the dazzling water;

divides and demarcates,
throwing an anchor through all liquid states.

XIII

Fingerlings of morning under shining water;
trout jumping through rain into the deepening stream.

In raw darkness, inevitabilities tumbling, clawing
the rough-smooth stones.

Slack muscles flowing
in quantities and quotients;

beyond recognizable surfaces,
obsessions, context.

Call me brother; tell me a lie; writing this,
hoping it isn't true.

In epiphany of all beginnings
only fingers are infinite.

XIV

Rise from your shadows.
Dream me into what you mean;

though you do not walk the water,
have no aptitude for miracles.

In turf of inner continents
slipping your glossy sensuous lips.

Shadows crawl on granite and pine,
jump through sunlit fingers.

I dreamed all night of horses,
luckywhite, velvet-eyed.

XVII

The forest turning beautiful with rain
curls into itself;

living between the hours and branches;
looking up, looking down, forgetting;

the end that is
segmentation of all beginnings.

In the fishtank of my head
the water bled.

The rain that will not let me die
sleeps.

XVIII

for my mother Marie

In the uncaged beauty of your wings
all things dwindle; oceans collide.

In the hulls of ships you sink
your fingertips. Above us lives the weather.

Ship-shaped and nameless, blowing on your own
breath
as death moves in it.

The feats of love drew us down
through the same occasions.

Beyond frail gestures your light
has its own voice.

XIX

for my mother Marie

Somewhere between the river and the sea
your blood waits listening;

reading your fingers like stars
along the dotted darkness of your arms;

your tongue on my *hello*
flashing through dreams like an arrow.

Dust of mercy, dust of grace,
dust from which you cover your face;

you leave what love loves best
and struggle with the rest.

XX

Under the ambush of waves
first light of morning.

The sun collects her debts
rendering all beggars unsuccessful lovers.

Your alibi silence
salutes into readiness.

Alchemy of belief; flame in fingers;
onion turned to gold.

The heart burns but is not burnt;
the tear gives off its fire.

XXI

The unconscious chatter of rain
refuses to be silenced.

You give too much, try too hard,
succeed only in undoing.

On days the sun does not shine, darkness
takes the heart into its country;

zero to zero; irreducible;
aces with their spades digging;

petals of forgotten poems
springing back from loam trembling.

Always the breath of lions
at the edge of things.

IV

Going Back

Shining in the wind
the horse and willow unfurling, glisten seaward
rising into vertical.

Forgetting what it was
that paved the way to silence —
words in anxious vials
stun the obvious — a paralytic needle
deeper than epiderm,
thirstier than the multicoloured birds
singing in the trees at sunrise.

In a dream a crow flies backwards
shining in the wind.

August Sun

The eyes inside my head are going
down to the sea in pennies
singing to all the little sad ships
where gods of air and weather stamp
light-heeled into waves,
splashing the air with their singing,
chanting prayers for the new sons of summer,
striding spidery skin.

Is a doctor on the loose
or merely gods working hard at dying,
picking through detritus —
less than this, more than that,
bouquet of bone, flash of blood?

Through hard light hammering the eyes
the heart holds its own darkness,
a vial of poison lining the skin.
Taut wires of sky reel down
in electric terrestrialities, sun-sworded
opacious energies flaming
toward a pointed pointlessness —
starlit and embryonic.

Maples in Fall

Trees walking the street
rub their roots along my back.

I feel naked under their delicate
root hairs. The street is full

of blowing leaves. I fear
their crisp impotence,

decay of red veins. Overhead
stripped limbs stretch in frigid air.

Each morning I carefully snip
white hairs from my head. Buds

swell already in the trees.

Tygers

Through sluices of summer
rainwater slides to be
whatever it is that makes a day

sing without sun and harbour rain,
float where the afternoon
leaves its stain on the hourglass,

squint through sunburnt eyes
blistering in speechless waxy forms
consciousness meanders and confirms.

Against fresh tracks
the rain makes
tigers of water ply their claws,

swirling through the drizzle
in separate membranes
swelling between consonant

and vowel, tongue and tooth.
Hunched in an afternoon of evenings
a generation of burning tigers

sinking their tongues in water
roar leaping into gutters.
In canyons of the mad

thundering as days grow old
the almanac's tough weather rips the skin
where the heart hides

in elliptical spaces
waiting,
fearful of their perfect symmetry.

Alien

A free gift left one night on the step
in a spice box branded with stars
and your plastic limbs afloat
in a styrofoam sphere.

Through liquid breath, hissing
the way eternity hisses
to spiral alone round invisible bones, and you
asleep in your distant world,
the moments of blood
flying unfathomable atoms
as flesh into pure consciousness descends
from steel to steam as the spirit
bends at the river's edge
crying.

And you work your words
with blood and spoon
through lips of bright water
where your lunar surfaces shine
along the scuttled particulars of time.

A free gift left one night on the step
in a spice box branded with stars
and you wake in the light
to find yourself

stepping toward the terrible empty shoes
through shadows of someone
you once knew.

Circus

The ghost of a circus circling
tightrope and trapeze,
the air swinging with bubbling muscle
glistening, leaps in the dome —
clowns falling off bikes
spinning in the path of white horses
where sequin-suited blonds
striding curving backs
above the whirring dust
as the substance of a moment glides
to great gray elephants
varoomphing round the ring
echoing entrances on quaking ground.

In the quiescent impulse
of a day miniaturised by memory,
a speck struts light
between the globes of rain
and tightroping a spider's moist thread
in stems of the wet grass,
holds the balance

until the splinters come
crawling from Heaven through the air,
trumpeting, resilient, marching
in soft brown motes
and flukes and filaments —

shadows spidering the grass
as each fragment of consciousness
shifts its shape to other things.

Instinctive

The genetics of self-recrimination
crystallize like frost
or the fist of an ancient god —

detritus of the soul
torn, frail as a denim shirt
stitched wild and bright with flowers.

Costlier by far
the habitat of these old remnants
drawn by blood,

these tired fingers marching in tens
up the steps of a new ark
seeking refuge where no refuge is,

stirring to the pulse and crush of water,
the tide's blood rising
into splintered consciousness,

this tunnelled cornea of light
diffused and clouded,
abstract and unforgiven, driven

by a monkey without a name
whirring round a tin cup on an organ
in a gold emblazoned fez.

Wolf Boy

In involuted spirals of howls and vowels,
the dog-faced boy screeches to

all his inebriate selves dwelling in
whatever it is he dances from, dances to,

dances in without ever arriving,
whatever he dances to be or not be.

Such is he that puppy dogs' tails
will not suffice, nor sugar, nor spice —

less substance, more desire,
backbone of the wind to drive him further

and fire of night to draw him back,
moisture of scar and distance

to settle whatever should not be disturbed.
In rituals of bone and trance

whatever it is he chants from, chants to,
chants in without ever arriving,

whatever he chants to be or not be,
hunting the dark forests

instinct knows his name
knowing less, feeling more,

unable to live by chance
and memory no longer any help.

Lilac

Outside the angry house
cyclone winds
whistle-whip the quiet silhouettes.

Glassy embers gesture and disappear.
Mutinies of flesh
thrust in volcanic cankers

to sword-tipped pluralities of time
to time talking —
God-mouthed rivulets silvering the air —

flicker of tumescent elements,
tongues tumbling through gold
from perfect mouths

of swimmers twitching into light,
of seismic voices, armoured roar and clatter
of screeching demons being squeezed

to puffs of leopard ghosts.

Swallows

The swallow zips and unzips clouds, zig
zagging tenderly in *oh my*
and *weeeee....* and *didyuseethat,*
bursting shadows in a whisper
wooshing through spoken undulations
passing through the head
faster than the speed of dark
and into clouds eating thin children
elongated by the sun.
                    In a picture
from Hiroshima a man's shadow
waits for a swallow that does not come,
does not fly past or through
his fiery head, and atomless since forty five
the shadow can't return so flies
blue across my China cup
dizzy with clouds.
                    Shadows zoom
through nettlebeds, boughs of Douglas fir, holly,
under water swimming with the perch,
in gray motions airily over fields,
but I will not let you in again
to rustle through my head,
your wings catching on old lace curtains
which used to screen you out.

What is it
moves in a shadow small as you, takes
its being from sun and air
flashing through dense objects
larger than the cat who stalks and falls
voluptuously for what
you cannot be?

Winter Fires

Sometimes the winter fires will do,
the wind with thin lips
blowing little skeletal things that once

were embryos on fire with time.
On dark bristling wings tipped with red
I crush an insect as I crush

all things I do not wish to know,
and you with your infrared evening face
say it is not so and I can no longer

borrow time with blindness.
Sometimes it's the passion that must
be left behind, or obsession

alone in its double cut and witless
fandango of wishes dreaming to life
what shadows dare not dare —

a witch pushing out of corners
wishing into each desire
the dark fire of things.

Max Plater, originally from England, was a social worker in the Vancouver area for some 20 years before becoming a teacher in Surrey, British Columbia, where he now lives. He has published in a variety of magazines in Canada and the United States. This is his first book of poems.